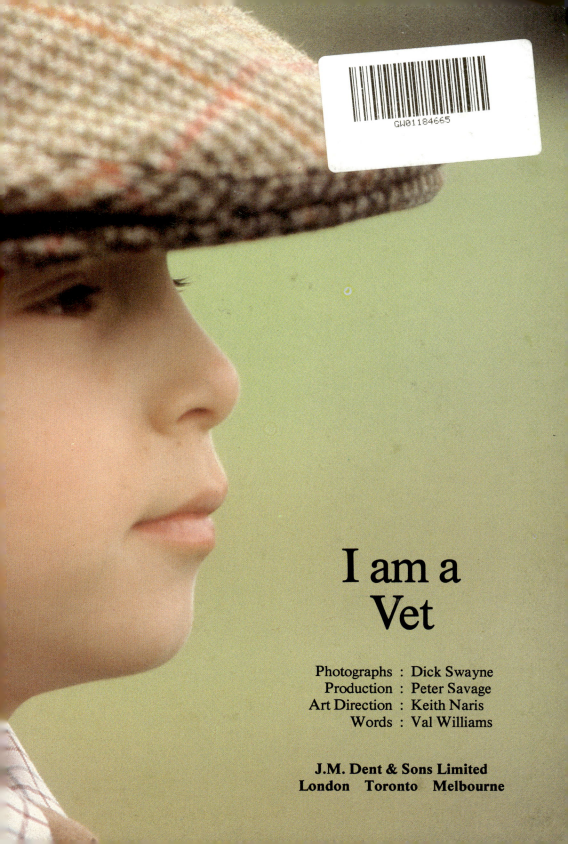

I am a Vet

Photographs : Dick Swayne
Production : Peter Savage
Art Direction : Keith Naris
Words : Val Williams

J.M. Dent & Sons Limited
London   Toronto   Melbourne

I am a vet. My name is Mark.

My first patient is Smokey. She has cut one of her paws. Before I look at the wound, I listen through my stethoscope to her breathing. Yes, she seems calm. Now, let's see to that paw.

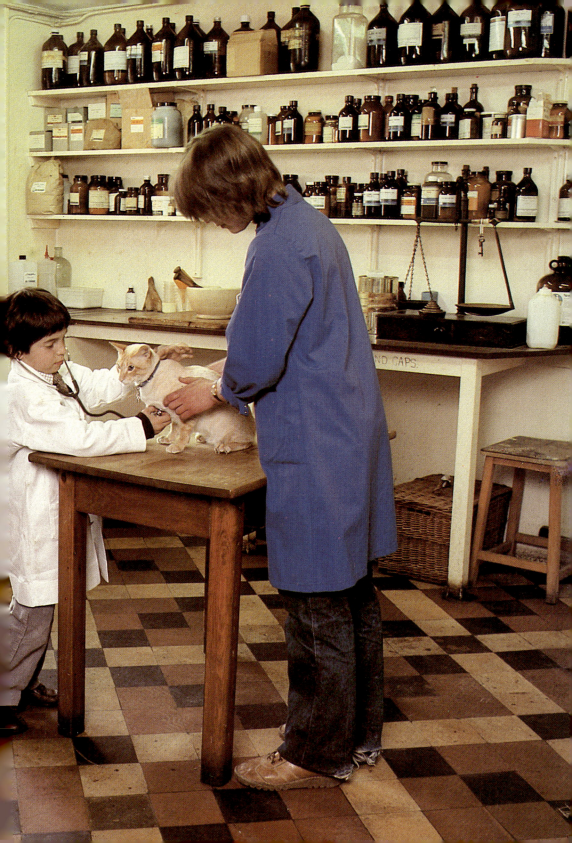

I clean the wound with anti-septic powder. Then I bandage it gently but firmly. 'Bring her back in a few days,' I say to the cat's owner.

This is my auroscope.
With its strong light,
I can see right inside
an animal's ear. Ah,
yes, this poor dog is
troubled by mites.
Special eardrops will
soon cure him.

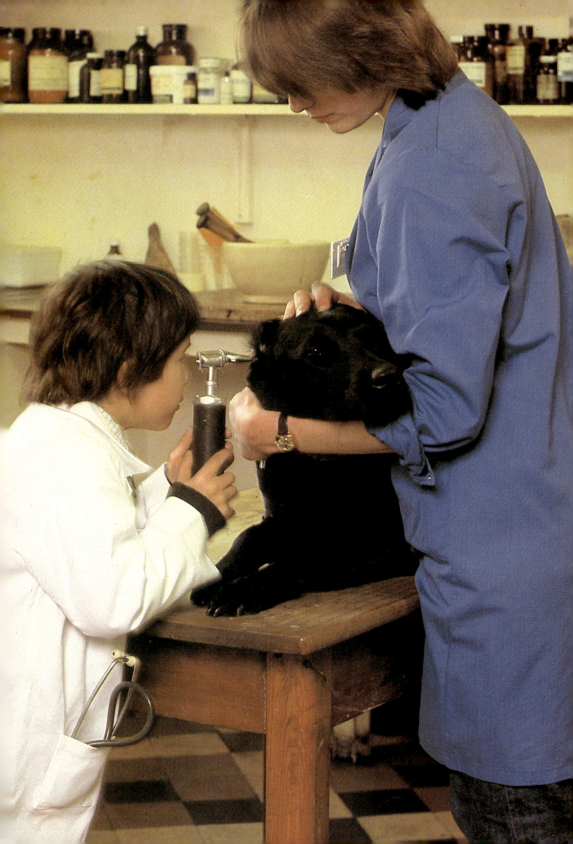

This is Rover.
I shall listen to his heart with the stethoscope.

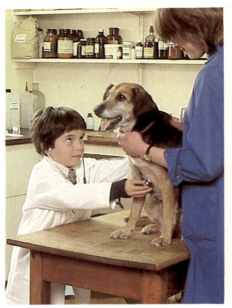
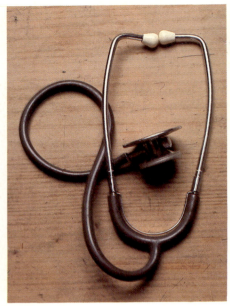

The tortoise has lost his appetite.
What he needs are vitamin drops.

Now I am studying germs under my microscope.

Most days start early for vets. I've just had a telephone call from a local farmer. He wants me to look at one of his lambs.

My bag's always packed. Nobody likes waiting long for the vet or doctor.

Sometimes a lamb has to be fed with a bottle, just like a baby. I test her legs, too. They seem fine.

I always say hello to Daisy.

She's a very good milker.

It's important for a farmer to have a good vet nearby. His animals can so easily be injured. I'm sure Mr Richardson will be calling me again before long – though not, I hope, quite so early in the morning!

Smokey's back again, so let's see how well her paw has healed.